Original title:
Oak Lore and More

Copyright © 2025 Creative Arts Management OÜ
All rights reserved.

Author: Oliver Bennett
ISBN HARDBACK: 978-1-80567-171-8
ISBN PAPERBACK: 978-1-80567-470-2

The Connection of Earth and Sky

A squirrel debates a wise old tree,
About who's taller, just for glee.
The roots roll eyes and start to giggle,
As branches sway, they dance and wiggle.

The clouds puff up with laughter too,
They drop some rain, oh, what a view!
The sun cracks jokes that brighten the ground,
While shadows stretch, they gather around.

Timeless Conversations in Green.

Two leaves gossip in a breezy chat,
"Did you see that squirrel? What a brat!"
A bug overhears and starts to hum,
"Let's start a band, this will be fun!"

The branches sway, they join the spree,
Barking dogs in the distance agree.
The flowers laugh, they twist and bend,
In nature's humor, all hearts blend.

Whispers of the Ancient Grove

In the heart of the grove, secrets abound,
Rabbits bicker over who's the fastest around.
The owls hoot softly, wise and sly,
As they pass the night with a twinkling eye.

The mushrooms chuckle, all draped in dew,
They tell tall tales, as fungi do.
While acorns drop with a plop and a thud,
"Hey, watch it!" crabs the earthworm with a thud.

Secrets Beneath the Canopy

Beneath the leaves, the critters compete,
For the title of the fastest on their feet.
The hedgehogs giggle, "Oh, what a sight!"
As snails take ages, "We're in no fright!"

They plot pranks on the unsuspecting fox,
"Let's hide his shoes, and swap his socks!"
But when the sun sets and the moon starts to glow,
They share stories of jest in a friendly show.

The Palette of Seasons

In springtime's charm, the buds unfold,
Colorful whispers, nature's gold.
Summer's hot sun, a sassy dance,
Sunburned squirrels, with a nutty prance.

Autumn's sassy breeze, leaves take flight,
Dressed in amber, a comical sight.
Winter's cold grip, trees wear their frown,
Snowmen giggle, in fluffy white gowns.

Guardians of the Green

Mighty trunks stand, with tales to spin,
Knocking acorns, let the mischief begin.
Branches stretch wide, sharing their cheer,
Bubbly chipmunks hold secret meet-ups near.

Frogs croak riddles, in muddy old ponds,
While wise old owls plot funny pronds.
Rabbits hop in, with jokes to unfold,
Nature's jesters, in mischief untold.

The Language of the Leaves

Whispering winds, have secrets to share,
Leaves rustle softly, a natural flair.
Branches high-five, in a leafy jest,
Nature's round table, with squirrels as guests.

Tickling breezes, giggle and tease,
Every flurry, a joke, sure to please.
Gossip of the forest, a leafy delight,
Every leaf's chuckle puts shadows to flight.

Chronicles of the Forest Floor

Beneath the giants, a bustling floor,
Busy bugs dance, in a frantic encore.
Fungi giggle, dressed in bright hues,
Sharing tales, of hapless, lost shoes.

Critters scurrying, with snacks to find,
One trips on a root, oh, how unkind!
Nature's drama, in the underbrush plays,
With laughter erupting, on sunny green days.

Beneath the Sheltering Leaves

In the shade of green, we picnic with glee,
Squirrels are laughing, oh what could it be?
Birds try to gossip, but who hears their song?
Under leafy cover, we'll dance all day long.

With sandwiches flying, and chips in the air,
A raccoon pops in, showing off his flair.
We giggle and chuckle, the world feels so bright,
Beneath all these leaves, everything feels right.

Mysteries of the Ancient Roots

Roots tangled deep, like an old family tree,
Whispers and secrets, oh, what could they be?
The ground is a story, each bump is a clue,
But don't ask the ants, they have nothing to do.

A snail moves in slow-mo, claiming his fame,
While worms weave their tales, none ever the same.
With a wink and a nod, the history flows,
In the dance of the soil, laughter softly grows.

The Reverent Silence of Trees

In the stillness of woods, where the tall ones reside,
They listen to secrets, with branches stretched wide.
A woodpecker knocks, it's his form of a joke,
While shadows take bets on the next sound to poke.

Leaves rustle softly, a chuckle's escape,
As squirrels take wagers on who'll steal the grape.
Nature's great choir, a hilarious show,
With punchlines unseen, only trees seem to know.

Serenade of the Swaying Limbs

With limbs in a jig, and roots in a twirl,
Branches are dancing, giving life a whirl.
The wind sings a tune, tickling bark just right,
As shadows keep rhythm, in the fading light.

Some critters join in, a concert of cheer,
While a butterfly flits, barely holding a beer.
Nature's own circus, with laughter and grace,
In this orchestra green, there's always a space.

Beneath the Boughs of Memory

Under branches wide and grand,
Old squirrels plot to take a stand.
With acorns bouncing off their heads,
They dream of more than cozy beds.

A crow caws loud, and what a fuss,
While rabbits race on whimsical bus.
Each tale they weave, a silly jest,
In the shade where laughter rests.

Glimmers of Sunlight's Touch

The sunbeam tickles leaves so bright,
While shadows dance in sheer delight.
A sloth struts by, so full of flair,
Declaring he's the fastest there!

The rabbit's laugh echoes through time,
As turtles claim the hills they climb.
Their secret pact, an age-old game,
Each chase a story, wild and tame.

Chronicles on the Forest Floor

A log rolls over, thinks it's spry,
Embarrassed when the roots reply.
'Why hurry, friend? Just take a seat!'
With bugs and pebbles at their feet.

The mushrooms chuckle, hats askew,
While singing deer share old déjà vu.
They toast with sap, their voices rise,
Nature's laughter fills the skies.

The Parables of the Grove

In a corner, wise old pine,
Speaks softly of the silliest wine.
"You'd think that grass could hold a grudge,
But listen close, it loves a judge!"

Each story spun beneath the boughs,
Where mischief brews and laughter prowls.
From feasting ants to frog charades,
The grove delights in all parades.

Echoes of the Timbered Past

Once stood a tree with dreams so high,
Winds would whisper secrets, oh my!
Squirrels plotted mischief in the boughs,
Chewing acorns and taking their vows.

Rabbits danced beneath the leaves,
Telling tall tales, oh how they weave!
A raccoon chimes in with a giggling tune,
While foxes debate who might visit soon.

Trees rolled their eyes at the antics below,
Holding their laughter in a trunk's proud show.
Each ring a story of folly and craze,
Nature's own sitcom, through centuries it plays.

At harvest time, they'd all join the fun,
Playing hide and seek, 'til the day was done!
Beneath the branches, life's laughter spread,
An echoing chorus of vibrant thread.

Beneath the Canopy's Watchful Eye

Beneath the leaves where shadows conspire,
A picnic was planned, oh what a fire!
But ants intercepted with a sly little scheme,
Sharing the crumbs—was it all a dream?

The sparrows squawked, divvying up bread,
While squirrels debated on who'd be fed.
All the while, the branches just shook,
In laughter and glee, in every nook.

Clouds above watched in wonder and glee,
As the creatures below sipped their tea.
A chorus of giggles filled the whole space,
Nature knotted together, a giggly embrace.

Suddenly a gust swooped down with a swirl,
Sending napkins flying—oh, what a whirl!
They laughed as they chased in a chaotic spree,
Beneath the great guardian, wild and free.

A Tapestry of Roots and Wings

Beneath the branches, the chatter was grand,
With butterflies flitting, life took command.
Worms spun tales deep down in the earth,
Of rivalries sprouting since the day of their birth.

The owls donned glasses, looking so wise,
While raccoons donned masks as their playful disguise.
Cardinals argued over the fanciest nest,
Mockingbird chimed in, accepting the test.

Tickling the roots with a mischievous vine,
The flowers laughed softly, feeling divine.
As echoes of laughter danced through the trees,
Nature's own comedy played in the breeze.

And when night blanketed all they could see,
They dimmed the lights, yeah, just let it be.
With chuckles and grins, as stars twinkled bright,
In this tapestry's weave, all felt just right.

Embrace of the Silent Sentinel

In the glade where shadows shift and sway,
Lived a sentinel who kept mischief at bay.
With branches like arms, it would reach and bend,
As critters plotted, the games would extend.

A hedgehog approached with a wink and a smile,
Proposing a race—he'd traverse quite a mile!
The deer rolled their eyes at the thought of a chase,
While the owl hooted softly, keeping the pace.

Together they giggled 'neath the ancient boughs,
As all of nature took part in its vows.
The tall tree just chuckled at their funny parade,
Rooted in laughter, their bonds were remade.

And when twilight fell with a warm, gentle sigh,
The sentinel smiled, watching stars dot the sky.
A playful embrace of the moments so sweet,
In that woodland world, where joy felt complete.

The Wisdom of the Rings

In the forest, rings so wide,
Whispers of ages, side by side.
Each notch a tale, some quite tall,
Of squirrels who thought they'd conquer all.

A little acorn, so proud and bold,
Once dreamed of growing, oh so old.
"I'll be a giant!" it would boast,
Now it's just some critter's toast.

A trunk so thick, a storybook,
With knots and grooves, just take a look.
Branches wave like hands in cheer,
To every silly tale we hear.

So gather 'round, take a seat,
Nature's punchlines can't be beat.
In every ring, a chuckle's found,
Where laughter grows on sacred ground.

Dance of the Wind and Leaves

The breeze is a jester, oh so spry,
Tickling the leaves as they whirl and fly.
"Catch me if you can!" they giggle and shout,
As butterflies join in, dancing about.

Dandelions puff, a fluffy parade,
With seeds like confetti, a jest well made.
Who knew the wind was a trickster grand?
Spreading laughter across the land.

The branches sway, in a merry jest,
Trees giggle softly, oh what a fest!
Birds drop their jokes from high above,
In their feathery world, full of love.

Under this canopy, wild and free,
Nature's comedy flows like tea.
So twirl and sway, let the fun commence,
In this playful stage, no need for tense.

The Old Sentinel's Reverie

With bark so gnarled, and wisdom vast,
The ancient tree recalls the past.
It dreams of days when sprigs were free,
And life was filled with mystery.

A rabbit once asked, "What's it like up there?"
The tree just chuckled, "More wind than hair!"
The squirrel's grand plans for acorn loot,
Always end with him falling, oh what a hoot!

"Tell us a secret!" the critters plead,
The old sentinel smirks, "Plant a seed!"
In every tale, a lesson is spun,
But mostly it's just about having fun.

So gather your friends, let stories unfold,
Around this wise tree, let laughter take hold.
For in its shade, the world seems bright,
And even the shadows dance with delight.

Canopy Conversations

Up in the branches, the gossip flows,
Leaves sharing secrets that only they know.
"Did you see that bird? What a silly flight!"
"More like a clumsy dance in broad daylight!"

The branches listen, with patient grace,
While twirling tendrils join the chase.
"Who knew a breeze could tickle so fine?
Let's laugh together, over cups of pine!"

"Remember that storm?" the elder wood quips,
"When we all swayed like we practiced our flips!"
The trees erupt in fits of mirth,
Recalling the chaos with playful girth.

So lean in close, let the laughter rise,
In every rustle, a sweet surprise.
Nature's banter is never a bore,
In this canopy, we always want more!

Songs of the Forest Sentinel

Beneath the boughs, they gossip, loud,
The critters gather, a raucous crowd.
A squirrel juggles acorns with glee,
While the owl hoots, "Look at me!"

The raccoon steals snacks in the night,
His masked face grinning, what a sight!
The trees shake leaves in laughter tall,
As critters dance and have a ball.

Chirping birds join in the fun,
Flapping wings, a wild run.
With every twist, the forest sings,
A merry tune, oh what joy it brings!

So listen close to their forest cheer,
In laughter's echo, the tales appear.
Beneath the branches, mischief reigns,
Where every critter dances and gains!

Echoes of the Leafy Giants

Tall and sturdy, they tower high,
With branches swaying in the sky.
One says, "I've heard the funniest joke!"
While others giggle, feeling bespoke.

A worm pretends to be king of the bark,
While ants march by, singing in the dark.
A breeze whispers secrets to the leaves,
As gossip spreads like webs from eaves.

"Did you hear?" says one to the next,
"The squirrels just had a nutty context!"
The trees shake their limbs with glee,
At the raucous tales of whimsy free.

So gather near, let laughter ring,
For in their shadows, the forest sings.
The giants may be old and wise,
But they sure enjoy a feathery surprise!

The Spiral of Seasons

Winter whispers, but spring loves to tease,
As flowers bloom with the greatest ease.
Summer struts, bright and glowy,
While autumn's leaves dance, twirl, and showy.

The acorns drop, a clattering thud,
As critters prepare for the coming flood.
"Don't rush!" shouts a beaver with flair,
"Take your time in this seasonal affair!"

The trees wear coats of every hue,
Laughing together at the sky so blue.
The sun winks down, casting a ray,
While shadows duck and play hideaway.

"Oh what a ride!" the seasons say,
A merry-go-round in a shadow play.
Each moment crafted with whimsy bright,
In the forest's heart, there's pure delight!

Tales from the Woodland Elder

Once there lived a wise old tree,
With stories tucked in each branch, you see.
He'd tell of squirrels and owls' debates,
And how laughter echoed through woodland gates.

"Gather around, you young sprigs," he'd call,
"Let me share the silliest tale of all.
Of a fox who wore a fancy hat,
And shouted, 'Look, I'm a courtly aristocrat!'"

The mushrooms chuckled, the ferns would sway,
As the elder spun stories both wild and gay.
"Just remember, laughter keeps us young,
So let it soar, let it be sung!"

With every tale, the woodland shined,
In the heart of nature, joy aligned.
For in the whispers of the leaves up high,
Lives the spirit of fun that can never die!

Shadows in the Glade

In the glade where shadows play,
Squirrels dance and shout hooray!
With acorns bouncing off their heads,
They trip and tumble, off their beds.

Mossy rocks become their stage,
A bobbing ballet, all the rage!
Mice are clapping, birds do cheer,
"Oh look! Here comes the fall, oh dear!"

The sun peeks in with a wink,
While beetles pause to stop and think.
A rabbit hops in disbelief,
"Is this a circus or a leaf?"

Yet in this fun of furry friends,
The laughter echoes, never ends.
In the shadow's play of light,
Nature giggles, oh what a sight!

Songs of the Swelling Knots

Beneath the trees with gnarly knots,
Lizards serenade their laughing thoughts.
Their tunes are silly, full of cheer,
"Watch out for the falling deer!"

The knots they swell, a bumpy ride,
A snail slips past, a bit of pride.
"I'm the fastest!" it declares,
While the birds chirp, "Who really cares?"

Acorns drop like drumbeats loud,
Trees sway gently, feeling proud.
"Did you hear the one about the stump?"
"Yeah, it tripped and made a thump!"

As twilight falls, the giggles rise,
A concert plays beneath the skies.
With every note, the forest thrums,
In knots of laughter, joy becomes!

Whirling Smoke and Canopy Dreams

In smoky swirls where dreams reside,
Chimneys puff and shadows glide.
A campfire crackles, sparks take flight,
"Who stole my marshmallows tonight?"

The canopy above whispers tales,
Of dancing leaves and giggling gales.
"Who knew trees could tell such jokes?"
"Maybe they're just playful folks!"

Squirrels leap on branches high,
While raccoons plot their midnight pie.
"Did you swap my snacks again?"
The trees whisper, "Oh, what a sin!"

In this tale of smoke and beams,
Where laughter mingles with the dreams.
Life spins on in nature's laughter,
A mystery we chase, ever after!

Dialogues of the Dappled Light

In the dappled light, a chat ensues,
Foxes gossip, swapping news.
"Did you hear about the frog?"
"He jumped so high, it stunk like fog!"

A wise old turtle makes his case,
"Keep your tales in slower pace!"
The shadows laugh and twirl about,
"Let's see who can shout the loudest out!"

With sunshine beaming through the leaves,
A rabbit boasts, "I've got my sleeves!"
"Who needs sleeves when you can hop?"
"Or dance around and never stop!"

In this theater of light and verse,
The woodland feels like a bustling universe.
With every quip and every jest,
Nature giggles, it's truly the best!

The Twine of Time

In the forest where whispers reside,
The trees tell tales, and they never hide.
I saw a squirrel with a top hat on,
He claimed he could dance 'til the break of dawn.

Time ticks slowly with laughter around,
As roots play tag under leaves on the ground.
A fox did a jig, and the owls all cheered,
I laughed so hard, I forgot what I feared.

The sun peeked through, as if to agree,
That life in the woods is a grand jamboree.
With twine of the past and laughter so sweet,
Every moment in nature is joyous and fleet.

So grab a twig, make a crown for your head,
And dance with the creatures, let laughter spread.
For time may untwine, but the fun will prevail,
In a world filled with magic and humor so frail.

Secrets of the Stalwart Bough

Upon the bough where the secrets lie,
A parrot winks with a twinkle in eye.
He squeaks of treasure buried deep in the bark,
But only at midnight, when it's time to embark.

There's wisdom in whispers, a chuckle so bold,
A wise old owl speaks of fables retold.
He claims he's a judge in feathered attire,
And every argument ends in a choir.

A squirrel with glasses, a scholar by trade,
Writes poems of acorns, in sun or in shade.
He says if you listen and giggle just right,
The trees will join in with their own little sights.

So gather around for stories and lore,
As the boughs sway with laughter, you'll ask for more.
With secrets unfolding as leaves rustle free,
Nature's got humor, just wait and see!

An Invitation to the Canopy

Hey there, friend, in the shade of the green,
The canopy calls, oh what a scene!
Join in the revelry, swing like the vines,
Where laughter floats up with the sweet southern pines.

The branches all chatter, gossip on the air,
'Did you see that raccoon with the flamboyant flair?'
He wore a new scarf, so bright and so bold,
Claiming fashion's a must, lest he seem old.

As sunlight dapples, let silliness reign,
With critters and giggles, it's never mundane.
A turtle in shades, cruising through the brush,
Claims he's the fastest… but oh, what a hush!

So come climb a branch, let's party and play,
In the heart of the trees, where we'll dance the day.
An invitation to joy, to laughter galore,
In the canopy's embrace, how could you ask for more?

The Forest's Hidden Heart

In the heart of the wood where the wild creatures play,
Lives a light-hearted spirit who brightens the day.
He's a badger in shades, expert in jam,
His dance moves are catchy, you'd call him a slam!

With leaves in his paws, he's the king of the funk,
He shakes his big tail where the mushrooms all clunk.
A rabbit, quite dapper, jumps in with flair,
Together they bounce, causing laughter to share.

The trees clap their hands, in rhythm they sway,
Join in their laughter, don't let it delay!
For the heart of the forest beats humor so light,
With every soft rustle, it's a tickle in flight.

So come one, come all, to this whimsical place,
Where pinecones are giggles and mischief's the chase.
In the forest's warm heart, let's frolic and cheer,
For nature's own humor is waiting right here!

Dreams Under the Linen Skies

Beneath the trees, a picnic spreads,
Squirrel debates with the crunchy bread.
A sandwich jokes, it starts to roll,
While ants gather 'round to take a stroll.

The moon peeks down with a silver grin,
As laughter echoes, where friends begin.
A napkin flutters, it waves hello,
While jellybeans dance with a cheeky bow.

A dream unfolds in a blanket's fold,
Of talking fruits, both brave and bold.
The lemonade giggles, tickling the bees,
As the sky blushes pink, 'neath the leafy trees.

In this jolly fest, where whims collide,
Every fruit and critter takes a ride.
So raise a toast, let joy amplify,
Under the linen, we laugh and fly!

The Timekeeper's Bough

Ticking clocks hang from the branches high,
While squirrels debate passing clouds in the sky.
A raccoon dons glasses, squinting at time,
Says, 'I prefer naps; those are sublime!'

The bees keep buzzing, timing their flight,
While butterflies waltz, avoiding the blight.
"Let's pause for a snack!" chirps an old crow,
As time slips away, like a well-timed show.

With cuckoo calls and a chime of delight,
The woodpecker rhythms take flight in the night.
"Oops! I forgot what I came here for!"
Sings a wise fox who was just passing by the door.

Underneath this bough, tales are spun,
Adventures await when the day is done.
So let laughter echo, let mischief thrive,
In this timeless realm, we're all alive!

Echoing with the Seasons

Spring whispers secrets in petals of hue,
While winter has snowballs, it knows what to do.
Summer's a jokester with ice cream in hand,
As autumn chuckles while dropping its stand.

Leaves throw confetti in colors galore,
While seeds have a party on the soft forest floor.
A rogue acorn rolls, causing quite the dance,
As branches sway gently, caught in a trance.

In this grove of giggles, the seasons all meet,
With laughter that lingers, oh, sweet and neat.
Rain showers tease with a tickling drip,
As clouds join in with a sassy flip.

Echoing stories of laughter and cheer,
In nature's embrace, all seem crystal clear.
So join in the revelry, sway with the breeze,
Where the seasons unite, doing just as they please!

The Treetop Testament

In the canopy high, where the owls conspire,
A charter of giggles is set to inspire.
The parrots squawk laws with flamboyant flair,
While the wise old turtle takes a comfy chair.

"Let's rule with joy, and laughter abound,
Skip nonsense and fuss; let freedom be found!"
A rabbit proposes, with carrots galore,
"Let snacks be our treaties, we all can explore!"

As critters convene for this festive decree,
They draft up some fun, as easy as can be.
"Every acorn's a treasure, protect it with pride,
For sharing our bounty keeps our joy multiplied!"

With chuckles and cheers, the verdict is passed,
This silly testament is sure to last.
So climb up the ladder, join this great fest,
For friendship means laughter, and that's for the best!

Tales of Terrestrial Time

In the forest long ago, with creatures so spry,
Squirrels told stories, I heard with a sigh.
They'd chatter and chuckle, plotting their pranks,
While trees raised their limbs, forming leafy ranks.

The mushrooms would giggle, their caps all aglow,
As bunnies hopped by, seeking trouble to sow.
A dance of mischief, shadows on ground,
In this woodland circus, joy could be found.

But wait, here comes Badger, with wise, furrowed brow,
"Stop all this frolicking! You're silly, I vow!"
Yet even he chuckled, cracked a soft grin,
In tales of the forest, laughter will win.

So if you seek fun in nature's embrace,
Just watch all the critters who race and who chase.
Each whisper and rustle, a joke on the breeze,
In the realm of the trees, there's humor to seize.

The Chronicle of Leaves

Once upon a time, in a leafy delight,
The leaves made a pact to play games out of sight.
The maples would tickle the oaks with their tips,
While birches threw parties with raucous quips.

The pinecones would dance on a breeze without care,
Claiming they'd float and be light as the air.
While ferns told tall tales of gnomes that they knew,
All gathering round for a whimsical brew.

"Who's the oldest here?" shouted a leaf from a larch,
"I'll spin you a yarn that will make your hearts arch!"
While the acorns giggled, and the chestnuts rolled,
In this forest of jest, being merry is gold.

So next time you wander where whispers abound,
Remember the laughter, the joy to be found.
Each leaf has a story, a quip to unfold,
In the Chronicle of Leaves, a treasure of old.

Remnants of Woodland Whispers

In the heart of the woods, where shadows play games,
The branches would gossip, puffing up their claims.
"Did you hear the tale of the raccoon's grand feast?"
"Or the squirrel who thought he was actually a beast?"

The toadstools conspired, plotting just out of view,
While the crickets chirped laughter, their tunes so askew.
A fox in her cunning, with secrets to share,
Spoke softly to all, with a mischievous flair.

"Woodland's got wisdom, wrapped up in its sway,
Listen close, and you'll hear what the twigs have to say!"
For every small whisper, likes to blend with the breeze,
Telling stories of joy through the rustling leaves.

So venture with glee, where the critters all meet,
Enjoy all the nonsense beneath your own feet.
In the remnants of whispers, you'll find pure delight,
With chuckles and tales as your forest invite.

The Spirit of the Canopy

High up in the branches, where the sun spills its gold,
The canopy dances, both lively and bold.
With shadows and giggles, the songbirds would tease,
As the squirrels performed their most daring of leaps.

"Why don't we hold a race, on this warm summer morn?"

Suggested the owl, while scratching a yawn.
With wings all-a-flutter, they lined up with flair,
Branches burst with laughter, up-high in the air.

A crow made a toast with an acorn in hand,
"Here's to our antics, so merry and grand!"
While the boughs gently shook, sharing sweet jokes,
In the spirit of canopy, the trees turned to folks.

So next time you're wandering and hear a soft laugh,
Know it's just nature, enjoying its craft.
The spirit of the canopy thrives in good cheer,
Where branches are friends, and the laughter feels near.

A Journey through the Timbers

Through leafy whispers, I did roam,
A squirrel threw acorns, claiming his home.
I tripped on a root, fell flat on my face,
The trees shook with laughter, what a funny place!

Each branch told a tale, though quite absurd,
A wise old owl, who was seldom heard.
He winked at me once, then pointed to bees,
"If they make you honey, you'll dance with the breeze!"

I chased after shadows, the shadows took flight,
Dancing around me till it turned dark at night.
A raccoon with a hat said, "You've lost your way,
But come join my party, we'll dance and we'll play!"

So, I slid down a trunk, quite slippery still,
And bumped into mushrooms, oh what a thrill!
With giggles of nature, my journey did end,
In the arms of the trees, where all joys blend.

Musings from the Hollow

In the heart of the woods, snug as a bug,
A rabbit wore glasses and gave me a shrug.
"Why don't you hop over and join the parade?
It's led by the hedgehogs, and they're never delayed!"

I pondered the quirks of the forest so dear,
While socks from a raccoon danced without fear.
The trees shared their secrets in whispers and laughs,
I wrote down their tales on a few leafy drafts.

A fox in a bow tie, oh what a sight!
Said, "Fashion's important, especially tonight!"
While the birds sang a chorus of songs so sweet,
I laughed at the jesters with two left feet.

But deep in the hollow, as twilight drew near,
The critters all gathered, and I could hear,
Their chuckles and jokes, so light and so free,
In a world made of wonder, just waiting for me!

Pathways among the Giants

Wandering paths where the giants stand tall,
A chipmunk in boots said, "Join us, or not at all!"
With mushrooms for hats, they marched in a row,
While I pondered their purpose and where they would go.

The shadows grew long, and the laughter began,
As the pine trees jived with a tap-dancing man.
A turtle in shades felt so cool on the stroll,
He winked at the moon, Oh, what a control!

By a brook made of giggles, we crafted a map,
With marshmallow islands and a chocolate trap.
The wind wagged its finger, "Oh, watch out for crumbs!
They'll summon the critters! You'll see, oh, the fun!"

A raccoon rode by on a bike full of cheer,
"Join us for a ride! The fun's over here!"
So, off we all zoomed, past the giants so grand,
In pathways of laughter, we went hand in hand.

Hushed Hymns of the Hollow

In the quiet of twilight, the shadows took flight,
A badger led hymns, echoed soft through the night.
With owls in formation, they flapped and they hooted,
Their songs were so funny, I nearly feuded!

The trees hummed along, with a rustle and sway,
Each branch added notes in a whimsical way.
A beetle on keys played a tune oh so sly,
Making everyone giggle beneath the night sky.

The squirrels held a nightcap with berries and cheese,
They toasted the stars, and they laughed with such ease.
While shadows of rabbits did swing from the boughs,
In the hush of the hollow, we all took our bows.

As the last note did fade, and the night turned to dawn,
I snuck out on tiptoe, but the humor went on.
In the laughter of trees, I'll forever recall,
The hymns sung in secret, the best time of all!

The Language of Leaves

Leaves whisper secrets, oh so sly,
Telling tales of birds that fly.
"Shh!" they giggle in the breeze,
As squirrels dance up the trees.

A rustle here, a murmur there,
Leaves gossip like they've got flair.
"Did you see the acorn's plight?"
"It dreamed of being a tree, so bright!"

Green thumbs poke and poke for clues,
Yet leaves just laugh, 'We hold the views!'
When branches sway, it's pure delight,
For trees hide secrets, out of sight.

In their shade, we ponder deep,
What do leaves know while we sleep?
In their dance, they tell me so,
In autumn's gold, they put on a show.

Emblems of Strength and Resilience

Beneath the bark, a tale unfolds,
Of battles fought and legends told.
Each ring a story, thick and thin,
Of weathered storms and strength within.

Saplings giggle, tall trees grin,
They've seen the sun, felt the wind.
A stumpy trunk will make you cheer,
"I'm here to stay, forget the fear!"

Roots deep down, they dance around,
Entangled friends in solid ground.
With every laugh and hearty quake,
They cheer each other for friendship's sake.

Old leaves chuckle, young buds tease,
"Let's face the winds like it's a breeze!"
Together they stand, sway and bend,
Nature's jesters, till the end.

The Cradle of History

In the shade of giants, stories grew,
Where little feet made whispers too.
Right below, a treasure's found,
With acorns hiding underground!

History giggles with each crack,
Of twigs that splinter, never lack.
"Remember that time we hid from rain?"
"I thought my bark would drive me insane!"

Little critters play their part,
In this forest, every heart.
From ancient tales to babbling streams,
Every branch holds enchanted dreams.

Underneath skies, both bright and gray,
The echoes of laughter lead the way.
Whispering trunks, a winking glance,
In the cradle of time, all trees dance.

Crowned in Autumn's Glory

A crown of colors, bold and bright,
Leaves wear their hues like sheer delight.
Pumpkin spice and apple cheer,
As the chilly winds draw near.

Squirrels scurry, branches sway,
"Let's collect our hat parade today!"
Falling leaves join in the fun,
"Catch me first, oh sneak, you run!"

In twirling reds and golden hues,
The trees throw parties, breaking news.
"Watch us party, take a peek!"
"Fall days are here, let's dance and squeak!"

A frolic here, a jump right there,
In autumn's breeze, we shed our care.
With laughter ringing, trees stand tall,
Crowned in glory, we love them all!

The Bark's Forgotten Tales

In a forest where whispers dwell,
The trees share secrets, can you tell?
A squirrel once claimed the crown of leaves,
While a rabbit danced, as the tree trunk heaves.

With bark that giggles and branches that creak,
They tell of parties held last week.
There's gossip of ferns that twirled for cheer,
But what the mushrooms know remains unclear!

A beetle dressed up in a tux of mud,
Promised to dance, but fell in a flood.
The wise old owl gave a hoot of pride,
As the woodpecker clucked, "Just take it in stride!"

So listen close, as the foliage grins,
Nature's a jokester, where laughter begins.
With tales of trees and creatures so spry,
You'll leave with a chuckle, oh me, oh my!

A Dance of Acorns

Underneath the canopy wide,
Acorns gather, full of pride.
They roll and tumble in a silly race,
Each one hoping to find a cozy place.

One acorn shouted, "I've got the moves!"
As the others laughed and tried to improve.
They spun in circles, then fell like rocks,
Creating a chaos that rattled the blocks!

A squirrel joined in, wearing a hat,
Claiming to be the best at combat.
But he fumbled and tumbled, lost his stance,
And ended up joining their wild, wacky dance.

With boisterous giggles and clattering sound,
The little nuts spun all around.
In the heart of the woods, where joy takes its reign,
Who knew doing the nutty twist could be such a gain!

Guardians of the Woodland

Gather 'round, dear creatures bold,
For a meeting of guardians, a sight to behold.
The frogs wear their hats, quite dapper and neat,
While the wise old deer taps a rhythm so sweet.

"Who guards the paths of giggles and glee?"
Quacked the ducks in a line, quite raucous, you see.
The fox said, "I'll keep the laughter intact,
Just throw in some puns, that's a fact!"

Then came the owls with their wide, wise eyes,
Adding more jokes, much to their surprise.
They hooted and hollered, and the mice squeaked loud,
As the woodland erupted, a laugher proud.

"Together we're strong, guardians of fun!
With giggles and chuckles, we'll never be done!"
So they kept the forest a joyous parade,
In the heart of the green, where friendships are made.

Timeless Shadows in the Forest

In the woods where shadows play,
Time giggles and runs away.
A hare tells tales to the passing breeze,
While the past is tickled in the rustling leaves.

"Did you hear of the tree that danced all night?"
Said a chipmunk with cheeks full of delight.
Its roots twist and twirl like they know the score,
While the brittle branches make the laughter roar.

A wise old fox with a glimmering eye,
Said shadows hold secrets, oh my, oh my!
"Why just last week, I saw a raccoon,
Debating the stars with a bright, merry tune."

Every corner, a chuckle, a grin appears near,
As nature tickles and fills up with cheer.
So dance with the shadows, embrace every whim,
For the forest is laughing, let's join in the hymn!

Nature's Sculptor

In the woodlands, trees do cheer,
With branches waving without a fear.
They tickle the clouds, play hide and seek,
And whisper secrets in language unique.

Squirrels in hats, oh what a sight,
Doing the tango in morning light.
A dance of leaves, they twist and shout,
Nature's party, without a doubt.

The Forest's Silent Scribe

The trees are scribes, they write so tall,
With bark and leaves, they cover it all.
If you listen close, you might just hear,
Their gossiping tales, full of cheer.

The rabbits giggle at their old jokes,
As wise owls roll eyes at the silly folks.
The pine trees shuffle, while birches sway,
It's a comedy show, come join the fray.

Storytelling Under the Stars

Under the twinkling blanket of night,
The fireflies gather, oh what a sight!
Telling tall tales of heroes bold,
And journeys of nuts—they're a sight to behold!

The moon cringes at the squirrel's tall claims,
While raccoons snicker, all playing games.
As stars take notes in their celestial glow,
The woods are alive with a joyful show.

Veins of Life in the Woodland

In the woodland's heart, a merry scene,
Where mushrooms wear crowns, all shiny and clean.
The roots intertwine, doing a jig,
While ants in tuxedos dance a small gig.

The streams chuckle softly, tickling the rocks,
As frogs in bow ties hop on their blocks.
The gnarled branches nod, a wise old crew,
In this wild theater, the fun never is through.

A Painter of Seasons

A brush dipped in sunshine, a splash of bright gold,
Leaves dance in the breeze, their stories unfold.
With each flick of the wrist, the colors will play,
Gathering giggles from the trees every day.

Winter paints white with a frosty embrace,
Snowmen slip and slide in a merry old race.
Spring paints in blush, with a wink and a cheer,
Tickling the petals, so bright and so clear.

Summer throws parties, each light is a guest,
With splashes of green, it feels like a fest.
Autumn hops in, with a shuffle and grin,
A palette of chaos, as leaves tumble in.

So here's to the painter, with laughter and glee,
Each season's a canvas, wild and carefree!

Yarn of the Woodland Spirits

In the heart of the woods where the laughter is loud,
Spirits spin tales beneath a leafy shroud.
They knit with the whispers of creatures so small,
Wool from the clouds, just a thread after all.

A squirrel pops in with a caper or two,
Stitching up stories with a nutty review.
Bears throw a party, resplendent in fluff,
While rabbits roll dice in a game that's quite tough.

With flutes made of twigs, they dance near the brook,
Their fashion's bizarre, just take a good look!
Socks full of acorns and hats made of moss,
In this woodland haven, no one feels loss.

So listen, dear friend, to the spirits at night,
Their laughter a chorus, so joyful, so light.

The Treetop Chronicles

Up in the branches, where the squirrels convene,
Lives a roguish raccoon, quite quirky and keen.
He jots down his tales on the bark of the trees,
Turning acorns to gold with the greatest of ease.

A parrot named Polly drops gossip galore,
About owls who snooze and the rabbits who snore.
Each cranny and nook, filled with laughter and fun,
As critters all gather to bask in the sun.

A gopher named George throws a pie in the air,
With laughter erupting, it creates quite a scare!
In this treetop saga where silliness reigns,
Adventure and whimsy sprout wild like the plains.

So climb up and join in, don't be shy, my friend,
For the tree's laughing magic will never quite end!

Whispers of the Wind

The wind carries secrets, in giggles, it hums,
Whirling through branches, it tickles and drums.
"Hey there!" it shouts, with a mischievous breeze,
"Catch me if you can, just follow the leaves!"

It teases the flowers, with a swirl and a spin,
Painting their petals with laughter within.
"Dance with me now!" it twirls through the glen,
A whimsical partner, again and again.

It whispers to critters, sharing cheeky tales,
Of raccoons in tuxedos and fluffy-tailed snails.
Each giggle a puff, as it whooshes along,
This merry old breeze is forever a song.

So next time you hear, that playful, soft sigh,
Know the wind is just giggling, floating on by!

Guardians of the Timbered Realm

In a forest where squirrels conspire,
Guardians gather, they never tire.
With capes made of leaves and hats of bark,
They plot their mischief from dawn till dark.

One spots a fox with a clever grin,
'Watch out!' they shout, 'He'll steal your pin!'
The owls hoot loud, trying not to laugh,
While the dogwood joins in with a clever quaff.

Under the moon, the shadows prance,
While critters hold their silly dance.
A raccoon slips and fumbles a snack,
'Whoops!' he cries, 'I'm under attack!'

So raise a glass of acorns, my friends,
To timbered tales that never end.
For laughter echoes through boughs and leaves,
In the woodland realm where humor weaves.

The Dance of the Swaying Boughs

Boughs sway gently in the breeze,
They giggle and wiggle with carefree ease.
A squirrel joins in, his tail a twirl,
While the branches bounce in a leafy whirl.

Up in the canopy, birds take flight,
Chirping rhymes that are quite a sight.
'Who's leading this dance? Is it you or me?'
'I lost my step, now I'm stuck in a tree!'

A wise old owl begins to sing,
Of days gone by and silly things.
'The trees have tales, so gather round,
For laughter hides where joy is found!'

So dance we will, till the sun goes down,
With leaves as crowns and smiles not frowns.
In this vibrant world of boughs untamed,
We'll sway and cheer, forever unframed.

Ink and Acorns

With ink and acorns, a tale unfolds,
Of woodland creatures and stories bold.
A raccoon scribbles, quill in paw,
'Look at my art!' with a mischievous draw.

Scribbles of mischief and playful cheer,
Make gullible critters all quake with fear.
'Beware the giant—oh dear, oh my!'
'A squirrel with a crown? That's just a lie!'

They plot and they plan, oh what a show,
With acorn hats they strut to and fro.
Page after page, the laughter cascades,
In their woodland world, no fear invades.

So here's to the artists beneath the trees,
With ink and acorns, we're never at ease.
A canvas of chaos, the fun never stops,
In this realm of humor, it happily pops!

Secrets of the Knotted Branches

Knotted branches whisper secrets old,
Of cheeky tales and legends bold.
A chipmunk listens, wide-eyed in awe,
At knots that twist like an ancient law.

'What's hidden here?' he asks in glee,
'Is it treasure, or maybe a key?'
The roots chuckle low, the leaves flutter near,
'Tis just tales of mishaps, no cause for fear!'

A wise old turtle, slow but spry,
Says 'Watch your step, or you'll surely fly!'
'With every twist and every turn,
Comes a lesson we all must learn.'

So linger awhile, let laughter reign,
As secrets unravel, time won't be vain.
In knotted branches, memories grow,
A whimsical world where fun steals the show.

The Enchanted Trunk

In the woods where whispers play,
A trunk once danced in bright ballet.
It tumbled down the hill with glee,
Shouting, 'Look at me, I'm free!'

A squirrel cheered from high above,
'Thank goodness you're not made of love!'
The trunk replied with cheeky flair,
'At least I don't have messy hair!'

Nearby a rabbit joined the game,
Said, 'Trunks like you are kind of lame.'
But with a laugh, the trunk rejoined,
'Friendship, dear, is what we coined!'

So they all danced till twilight came,
With laughter echoing through the frame.
A silly sight, oh what a spree,
In the woods, so wild and free!

Songs of the Rustling Foliage

The leaves began their vibrant croon,
Beneath the giggling, cheeky moon.
'Twiggy, don't sway, you're off the beat!'
'But I like to dance on tree-top's seat!'

The branches chuckled in delight,
As acorns fell with all their might.
'Careful now, you clumsy nut!'
'Whoops! Did I land straight on your gut?'

The foliage hummed a lively tune,
While crickets joined, 'We want a boon!'
And all together, they did sing,
'Nature's party is the best thing!'

So every night, a concert starts,
With fluttering leaves and joyful arts.
In whispers soft, they share their fun,
A symphony of not-so-quiet run.

Echoes of Roots Deep

Beneath the soil, where roots entwine,
A meeting place, oh how divine!
'Hey there, buddy, can you hear?
Let's spread some gossip far and near!'

The mushrooms listened, all agog,
As roots recounted tales by bog.
'Whoa, did you see that sapling dance?
It tripped on its own little prance!'

They chuckled hard, almost in tears,
With whispers swirling, loud cheers.
'We're all connected, it's really sweet,
In this grand web, we all compete!'

So here they laughed, as time went on,
Echoes of roots, under dawn.
Nature's jesters, growing tall,
In the soil, it's a ball!

The Spirit of the Timbers

Deep in the heart of the forest prime,
A spirit chuckled, what a time!
'Watch out for that tree-mendous spree,
They think they're wise, but they're just silly!'

The critters danced, unearthed some pranks,
With wooden jokes and laughter ranks.
'Hey, Mr. Pine, your bark's too loud!
Keep it down, don't tempt the crowd!'

The branchy folk would roll their eyes,
But clever tricks led to surprise.
They'd rig up swings and stunts galore,
Closing the gap, oh, what a score!

And as the sun began to set,
The timber spirit laughed, you bet!
In every creak, a giggle grows,
The jovial woods, where humor flows!

Echoes of the Elder Tree

In the forest, trees like chatter,
With squirrels talking, just like patter.
They giggle and gossip, quite a show,
While birds drop notes, 'Hey, watch me go!'

The elder tree nods, quite amused,
At tales of acorns and how they've fused.
"I once had a branch that danced with the wind,
Thought I'd fall over, but I just grinned!"

Raccoons roll by, wearing their masks,
Singing of mischief—oh, what a task!
The elder chuckles, "You little rascals,
Keep it down! You're shaking my bristles!"

From stories of roots to leaves on the keep,
In this timbered world, secrets run deep.
So next time you wander, just stop and hear,
The laughter of trees, they hold dear!"

The Heartbeat of the Timber

Beneath the bark, a party arises,
With critters counting, they roll double dice.
"Who's got the acorns? I've got some nuts!
Let's play charades in our cozy ruts!"

The trees hum along to the forest beat,
While rabbits hop in rhythm, such a treat.
Beetles do backflips, oh what a sight,
As fireflies buzz around, lighting the night!

But wait—oh no! The owls begin to hoot,
"Quiet down, everyone! I'm trying to snoot!"
The trees shake their branches, trying to scold,
"Reserving the silence, that's the old mold!"

Yet laughter erupts in the heart of the wild,
As critters protest, like rambunctious child.
In this timberland, joy finds a way,
Where even the branches join in the play!

Tales from the Gnarled Branches

In a nook of the woods, tales twist and twine,
Gnarled branches whisper with secrets so fine.
"Once I was a sapling, fresh and spry,
Now I see squirrels acting much too sly!"

A crow caws loudly, "What's this I hear?
Is it storytime, or time for a beer?"
The branches sway, "Oh, let's make it fun,
Pour me some shade when the day is done!"

The owl shrugs, "I'm far too wise for that,
But I'll spin a yarn, just tip my hat."
With laughter and echoes of woodland cheer,
The gnarled ones giggle—it's their time of year!

As nightfall drapes its silken thread,
Mischievous stories rise from each head.
These branches recall a life full of jest,
Their humor brings warmth, we're truly blessed!

Leaves of Legend

Each leaf tells a story, hang on to your hats,
From squirrels in dance to the wily chitchats.
"I was once a sprout, got blown off my perch,
Now I'm part of legends, call me the birch!"

Autumn comes calling, the colors delight,
Frogs leap for joy, giving quite a fright.
"Come join us!" they shout, "Let's have a grand ball,
With leaves swirling down, we'll have a great haul!"

Gusts tease the branches, causing them to sway,
Echoes of laughter brighten the fray.
"My uncle was a leaf in a parade, you see,
Dressed up as a taco, now that's quite a spree!"

So when you venture beneath the green crown,
Listen for giggles that dance all around.
For the leaves, they know where the wild stories roam,
And every rustle sings, "Welcome! You're home!"

Enigmas of the Understory

Beneath the branches, shadows play,
The squirrels plot their grand display.
They chatter loud, with nutty dreams,
   Conspiring under leafy beams.

The mushrooms giggle, sprouting bright,
They think they're wise, oh what a sight!
But all their secrets start to fade,
As rain comes down, their plans betrayed.

A snail slicks past, slow as can be,
Claiming it's time for a grand decree.
With every inch, it stops to pose,
Pretending it's the fastest, who knows?

Yet in this world, so wily and weird,
Each creature thinks it's truly revered.
With laughter echoing in the leaves,
  The understory is full of thieves.

The Dance of the Swaying Bark

A tree once thought it could just sway,
And led the breeze in a funny ballet.
With winds that kicked up a frassy jig,
The neighbors laughed, but weren't too big.

The roots all tapped, with rhythm intact,
While leaves clapped hands – a leafy pact!
A raccoon joined, all dressed in black,
Said, "I'm the star of this crazy knack!"

Around they twirled, a humorous blaze,
While critters cheered in a wild craze.
One branch took a bow, proud as can be,
While mossy mats grinned in glee.

But when the storm rolled in with flair,
They tumbled down, oh what a scare!
Yet in the aftermath, they stayed and laughed,
For friendship's the best and the funniest craft.

The Cerulean Sky Above

With clouds like fluff, the blue holds sway,
Birds argue o'er whose turn to play.
One claims it's time for a lovely song,
While another insists it's all gone wrong.

An owl up high, all dressed in gray,
Pretends to be wise, but likes to sway.
"Up here," it hoots, "the world's a stage!"
As clouds roll by like a funny page.

Thunder grumbles in a curious tone,
While lightning flashes, making it known.
The sky's just dressing for a big parade,
With antics that even the sun has made.

So next time you glance at that cerulean hue,
Remember it laughs at everything too!
With each flicker and roll, it's clear to see,
The sky's the biggest jester, wild and free!

Twisted Echoes of the Past

Once a knot told tales of old,
Of knights and quests and hearts so bold.
But every fiber, before you think,
Was packed with secrets, just on the brink.

In a twist, it shared a joke divine,
Of a bear who thought he was a fine wine.
He'd swish and swirl, with a haughty stare,
Then trip and tumble, no style to spare.

The woodpecker listened, cocked his head,
While all the branches shook with dread.
For laughter echoed in canopies vast,
Of all the silly things from times past.

So as you stroll through this twisted game,
Know every knot holds a blushing name.
With echoes of laughter wrapped in the bark,
Life's a giggle, just look for the spark!

Legends Written in Bark

In the woods where squirrels chatter,
Whispers of trees make hearts flutter.
A raccoon with a crown of leaves,
Proclaims the secrets no one believes.

The ants hold meetings under the sun,
Declaring that their work is never done.
A beetle wears glasses, looking quite wise,
Sipping dew drops under clear skies.

Robin Hood's arrow stuck in a trunk,
And a mole who thinks he's a punk.
Each groove in the bark holds stories galore,
Yet most folks just ignore and bore.

So be sure to listen next time you roam,
For the forest has tales to call its home.
Adventurers, gather, let laughter resound,
In the tales woven here, joy can be found.

The Embrace of the Forest Floor

Oh, the forest floor, a cushy bed,
Where mushrooms dance, and fairies tread.
A raccoon recites Shakespeare in jest,
While rabbits debate who's the best-dressed.

The leaves are confetti after a storm,
Snakes are slipping, oh, so warm.
A snail hosts a race, but oh so slow,
Cheering for friends, with a twinkle and glow.

A hedgehog holds court with all of his kind,
Revealing the gym secrets of the whole forest blind.
Each berry patch offers a juicy tease,
While squirrels compete for the highest of trees.

So come, take a tumble, embrace the fun,
Let your shoes get muddy, bask in the sun.
The floor of the forest, stories untold,
Where laughter and friendship simply unfold.

A Tapestry of Twigs

In a world full of twigs, a jigsaw of fun,
Where squirrels weave tales 'til the day is done.
An owl slips notes, quite proud of their rhyme,
While crickets keep rhythm, marking the time.

A kitten climbs high, then falls with a squeak,
Landing smack in a pile, looking quite meek.
Beetles put on a play, lighting it bright,
As fireflies dance, igniting the night.

The stitches of nature, tangled and wide,
Where each little creature has joy as their guide.
A badger reads maps with great, goofy flair,
While tree stumps hold meetings in their buttoned-up chairs.

So gather your friends, let's venture anew,
To a twiggish wonderland where laughter ensues.
Each twist and each turn, oh, what a delight,
In a tapestry woven by day into night.

Reveries at Dusk

As evening drapes its silken embrace,
Creatures gather, each finding their place.
A chorus of crickets, a serenade sweet,
While hedgehogs and owls tap dance their feet.

The moonlight spills secrets, softly they glow,
A porcupine tells tales of lovesick woe.
A minty breeze carries laughter and cheer,
While the cool of the night makes every heart near.

Squirrels share stories of acorns and dreams,
Yelling out punchlines and planning their schemes.
The starlit sky, a canvas to paint,
A mosaic of mirth, without an ounce of restraint.

So join in the fun of such reverent dusk,
Where every soft chatter reveals life's sweet musk.
In shadows and sparkles, with smiles untold,
The twilight whispers of adventures bold.

The Oak's Embrace

In the shade of a giant, I sat down to think,
Wondering how squirrels can so deftly wink.
Branches like arms wrap me in their cheer,
As I chuckle at nutty ideas, oh dear!

The leaves whisper secrets, a playful tease,
While acorns fall softly, aiming for knees.
I dodge and I weave, it's a hilarious game,
Nature's own version of hide-and-seek fame.

With each gust of wind, the tree seems to dance,
A jig of delight, perhaps a romance?
I swear that it giggles, a laugh so profound,
As birds join the fun, chirping all around.

In this lively embrace, I could linger all day,
Under the watch of the wise, leafy sway.
With humor intact, I take my sweet leave,
Knowing my friend's laughter, I shall always believe.

Memories in the Hollow Trunk

At the heart of the grove, there's a trunk with a grin,
Where stories are whispered, and dreams sneak in.
A hollow that bounces, each word like a ball,
And giggling old echoes just beckon my call.

I peek in the hole, what quirky sights there,
Beetles in tuxedos, preparing to share.
They laugh as they bumble, adjusting their ties,
Reminding me sweetly, the fun never dies.

With each little rustle, I giggle along,
The memories swirling, like a whimsical song.
A tale of a squirrel who fumbled his stash,
And fell on his face, oh, what a fine crash!

As shadows grow long, and the sun starts to set,
I'll treasure each chuckle, not one I regret.
For in this old trunk, there's magic galore,
A world filled with laughter, who could ask for more?

Guardians of the Sunlit Glade

In the bright, dappled light where the laughter is loud,
The guardians gather, a whimsical crowd.
With hats made of leaves and smiles that glow,
They dance 'round the glade in a comical show.

A chipmunk with swagger leads them along,
Singing out tunes with a voice so strong.
The rabbits keep rhythm with hops oh-so-daring,
While badgers roll over, quite happily sharing.

The sun peeks through branches, a spotlight on fun,
As flowers all giggle, petals come undone.
Through beams of bright laughter, the day marches on,
In a festival of joy, from dusk until dawn.

With each twirl and twist, they defy every rule,
Creating a scene that's wonderfully cool.
So if you wander near when the day's at its best,
Join in the revels, you're warmly blessed!

Stories Woven in Shadows

Beneath the old canopy, where shadows do play,
I found a sly fox who had something to say.
"Come closer, dear friend, for I've tales to spin,
Of mischief and mayhem where laughter begins!"

The whispers of old trees dance through the dusk,
With stories of critters and odors of musk.
From raccoons who rummaged to owls who confused,
Each tale had a twist, laughter expertly used.

The moon joined the party, a bright, watchful eye,
As shadows leapt higher, reaching the sky.
A chorus of giggles from unseen friends,
Woven through branches where silliness blends.

In the fabric of night, these stories shall weave,
A tapestry rich, as we laugh and believe.
For every old shadow has laughter inside,
A joy that invites us, a whimsical ride.

www.ingramcontent.com/pod-product-compliance
Lightning Source LLC
Chambersburg PA
CBHW070750220426
43209CB00083B/396